COUNTRY PROFILES

AUSTRIA

BY ALICIA Z. KLEPEIS

BELLWETHER MEDIA • MINNEAPOLIS, MN

Blastoff! Discovery launches a new mission: reading to learn. Filled with facts and features, each book offers you an exciting new world to explore!

BLASTOFF! UNIVERSE

BLASTOFF! Beginners — GRADE K

BLASTOFF! READERS — GRADES 1-3

BLASTOFF! DISCOVERY — GRADE 4

This edition first published in 2022 by Bellwether Media, Inc.

No part of this publication may be reproduced in whole or in part without written permission of the publisher.
For information regarding permission, write to Bellwether Media, Inc.,
Attention: Permissions Department,
6012 Blue Circle Drive, Minnetonka, MN 55343.

Library of Congress Cataloging-in-Publication Data

Names: Klepeis, Alicia, 1971- author.
Title: Austria / by Alicia Z. Klepeis.
Description: Minneapolis, MN : Bellwether Media, Inc., 2022. |
    Series: Blastoff! Discovery: Country Profiles | Includes
    bibliographical references and index. |
Audience: Ages 7-13 | Audience: Grades 4-6 | Summary: "Engaging
    images accompany information about Austria. The combination of
    high-interest subject matter and narrative text is intended for students
    in grades 3 through 8"– Provided by publisher.
Identifiers: LCCN 2021051723 (print) | LCCN 2021051724 (ebook)
    | ISBN 9781644876091 (library binding) |
    ISBN 9781648346200 (ebook)
Subjects: LCSH: Austria–Juvenile literature.
Classification: LCC DB17 .K52 2022 (print) | LCC DB17 (ebook) |
    DDC 943.6–dc23/eng/20211101
LC record available at https://lccn.loc.gov/2021051723
LC ebook record available at https://lccn.loc.gov/2021051724

Editor: Kieran Downs   Designer: Laura Sowers

Printed in the United States of America, North Mankato, MN.

TABLE OF CONTENTS

SCHÖNBRUNN PALACE

On a sunny summer morning, a family boards a sightseeing bus in Vienna. From the top deck of the bus, they see sailboats gliding on the Danube River. They stop to visit St. Stephen's Cathedral. Inside are colorful stained-glass windows and beautiful paintings.

OTHER TOP SITES

HALLSTATT

HOHE TAUERN NATIONAL PARK

HOHENSALZBURG FORTRESS

MELK ABBEY

Next, the family tours Schönbrunn Palace. It has more than 1,400 rooms and apartments. They wander through a maze in the palace gardens. It is made of tall hedges. Then, the bus brings the family to the city center. They eat soup with dumplings at a sidewalk café as the sun sets. Welcome to Austria!

Austria is located in central Europe. It covers an area of 32,383 square miles (83,871 square kilometers). The nation's capital is Vienna. It stands on the Danube River in the northeast.

Austria is **landlocked**. It does not touch any seas or oceans. It borders eight countries. To the north are Germany and the Czech Republic. Its eastern neighbors are Slovakia and Hungary. Slovenia and Italy border Austria to the south. Switzerland and the very small country of Liechtenstein lie to the west.

LIECHTENSTEIN

SWITZERLAND

CZECH REPUBLIC

GERMANY

SLOVAKIA

LINZ

SALZBURG

VIENNA

AUSTRIA

INNSBRUCK

GRAZ

HUNGARY

ITALY

SLOVENIA

LANDSCAPE AND CLIMATE

More than half of Austria is covered by the Alps. These mountains begin in the west and stretch through much of southern and central Austria. Tucked in these mountains is the Pasterze **Glacier**, the largest of many in the country. Rolling green hills lie north of the Alps while lowlands blanket much of eastern Austria. The Danube River winds its way through northern Austria and into Slovakia.

N
W + E
S

DANUBE RIVER

= ALPS
= PASTERZE GLACIER

FANTASTIC FORESTS

Austria is one of Europe's most wooded nations. Forests cover nearly half the country!

ALPS

VIENNA
Average
seasonal highs
and lows

JANUARY
HIGH: 39 °F (4 °C)
LOW: 32 °F (0 °C)

APRIL
HIGH: 63 °F (17 °C)
LOW: 48 °F (9 °C)

JULY
HIGH: 81 °F (27 °C)
LOW: 65 °F (18 °C)

OCTOBER
HIGH: 59 °F (15 °C)
LOW: 48 °F (9 °C)

°F = degrees Fahrenheit
°C = degrees Celsius

Austria has a **continental** climate. Winters are cold.
Snow covers the mountains. Rain often falls in the eastern
lowlands and in western Austria. Summers are mild.
In the east, there are much larger changes in temperature
throughout the year.

In Austria's alpine regions, furry marmots pop out from their underground burrows in search of food. Ibex and chamois move up and down the uneven slopes with ease. Yellow-billed choughs and eagles soar overhead. They dive down to grab reptiles or rodents.

A huge variety of birds make their homes in the reed beds of Neusiedler Lake in eastern Austria. Male great bustards perform dances to attract mates. Eurasian hoopoes use their long beaks to catch insects. Pike, perch, and carp swim in the lake's waters.

IBEX

NORTHERN PIKE

GREAT BUSTARD

ALPINE MARMOT

GOLDEN EAGLE

EURASIAN HOOPOE

EURASIAN HOOPOE

Life Span: **10 years**
Red List Status: **least concern**

Eurasian hoopoe range = ▮

LEAST CONCERN	NEAR THREATENED	VULNERABLE	ENDANGERED	CRITICALLY ENDANGERED	EXTINCT IN THE WILD	EXTINCT
▲						

VIENNA

Nearly 9 million people live in Austria. More than 8 out of 10 belong to the Austrian **ethnic** group. Germans make up the second-largest group. People from Bosnia and Herzegovina, Turkey, Serbia, and Romania also make up parts of the population.

More than two out of three Austrians are Christians. A smaller number are Muslim. But many people do not practice any religion. Most Austrians speak German, the country's official language. Croatian, Slovene, and Hungarian are also official languages in certain Austrian states.

FAMOUS FACE

Name: Arnold Schwarzenegger
Birthday: July 30, 1947
Hometown: Thal, Austria
Famous for: Award-winning actor, bodybuilder, and former governor of California

SPEAK GERMAN

ENGLISH	GERMAN	HOW TO SAY IT
hello	hallo	HA-lo
goodbye	auf wiedersehen	owf VEE-der-zane
please	bitte	BIT-eh
thank you	danke	DAHNK-eh
yes	ja	YAH
no	nein	NINE

INNSBRUCK

STREETCAR
VIENNA

Almost 6 out of 10 Austrians live in **urban** areas. Vienna is the biggest city in Austria. Nearly 2 million people live there. Most city dwellers live in apartment buildings or **row houses**. People often get around by bus, **streetcar**, subway, or car.

In the countryside, people often travel by bus or train. Car-sharing is becoming more popular in **rural** areas. It is common for rural Austrians to live in single-family homes. They are often made of stone, brick and plaster, or wood. Brightly colored window shutters and flower boxes decorate many homes.

GREEN HOUSES

Austria's government has set a goal of putting solar panels on 1 million homes by 2030. The country aims to get all of its electricity from renewable sources by this time.

Music is important to Austria. The country's rich musical **traditions** include folk music. A popular folk instrument is the *hackbrett*. Many villages have their own bands. Cities typically have professional orchestras that play classical music. Many people consider the Vienna Philharmonic to be one of the best in the world. Vienna even has an orchestra that only plays instruments made from vegetables!

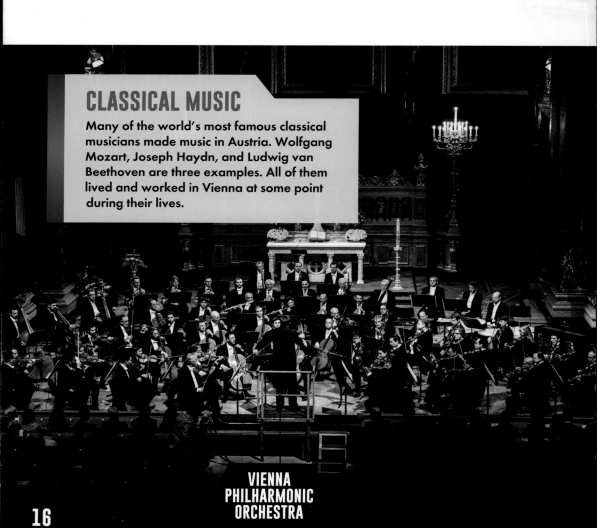

CLASSICAL MUSIC

Many of the world's most famous classical musicians made music in Austria. Wolfgang Mozart, Joseph Haydn, and Ludwig van Beethoven are three examples. All of them lived and worked in Vienna at some point during their lives.

VIENNA PHILHARMONIC ORCHESTRA

DIRNDLS

Austrians may wear traditional clothing for special events. *Dirndls* are colorful dresses with aprons worn by Austrian women. Today, waitresses or others in the **tourism** industry may wear dirndls. Mens' traditional dress includes *lederhosen*, or leather shorts often with suspenders.

Children in Austria must go to school from ages 6 to 15. During the four years of primary school, students learn math, reading, and writing. They also start learning a foreign language. Austria offers different types of secondary schools. Some young people learn specific job skills in **apprenticeships**. Others stay in school and may go on to university.

Nearly three out of four Austrians have **service jobs**. Some work in banks or health care. The tourism industry also employs many people. Austrian factories make iron, steel, machinery, cars, and chemicals. The nation's farms grow sugar beets, barley, and wheat.

CAR FACTORY

FARMING

SKIING

VACATION TIME

All Austrian workers get at least five weeks of paid vacation each year. In addition to exploring their home country, Austrians often travel abroad. Popular destinations include Italy, Greece, and Croatia.

Soccer is a popular sport in Austria. People play all across the country. Austrians also enjoy tennis, handball, and volleyball. Swimming and sailing are common outdoor activities. Winter sports are well-loved in Austria. Many people play hockey and ice-skate. Austrians also ski, snowboard, and hike in the mountains.

SOCCER

Each summer, people of all ages attend performances at the Salzburg Festival. Musical theater, operas, and dramas are all part of the events. Austrians also visit galleries and museums that display works by Austrian artists such as Gustav Klimt and Tina Blau.

MAKE AN ALPINE (TYROLEAN) HAT

Tyrol is a mountainous region in western Austria. This area is known for its green hats. They are often often made of wool and decorated with a feather.

What You Need:

- 12x18-inch construction paper (heavyweight is better)
- glue
- two small clips
- scissors
- craft feather
- elastic string

Instructions:

1. With the long edge of the paper at the bottom, fold your paper in half from left to right.

2. Turn your paper so the fold is at the top. Fold the top corners down to the center.

3. At the bottom of your paper below the triangle shape you created, fold up the top layer of the long flap. Flip your hat over and fold up the other flap.

4. Fold in the corners of the flaps so that they are in line with the triangle shape of the hat. Glue the corners down. Place one clip over each of the corners and leave in place until the glue is dry.

5. Glue a feather to your hat.

6. Use your scissors to make a small hole in the center of the bottom of each side of your hat. Thread some elastic string through the holes and adjust to fit under your chin. Tie a knot on each side to keep the string in place. Enjoy wearing your alpine hat!

Breakfast can vary widely in Austria. Some people eat bread rolls, or *semmel*, with butter and coffee. *Tiroler gröstl* is traditional in the Tyrol region. It is made of fried potatoes, bacon, and onions, topped with a fried egg. For other meals, Austrians may eat breaded **veal** cutlets known as *wiener schnitzel*. Dumplings called *knödel* are often served with soup.

Austrian desserts are well-known around the globe. *Sachertorte* is a rich chocolate cake with layers of apricot jam inside. Apple strudel is another sweet treat. It is dusted with powdered sugar and contains apples, raisins, and spices.

WIENER SCHNITZEL

SACHERTORTE

KAISERSCHMARRN

Start your day off with these tasty and traditional Austrian pancakes. Have an adult help you make them.

Ingredients:

4 eggs, separated into yolks and whites

1/2 cup milk

3/4 cup flour

1 teaspoon baking powder

2 tablespoons sugar

1 pinch salt

1/3 cup raisins

4 tablespoons butter, divided

Steps:

1. In a big bowl, combine egg yolks, milk, flour, baking powder, sugar, and salt until mixed well. Let this mixture sit for 10 minutes.

2. In another bowl, use a hand mixer to beat the egg whites until they are stiff.

3. Gently fold the egg whites into your batter. Gently add the raisins to this mixture.

4. Melt two tablespoons of the butter in a frying pan over medium heat. Pour the batter into the pan and cook until the bottom looks slightly golden. This should take about six to eight minutes.

5. Place the pancake onto a plate with the cooked side down. Add the rest of the butter to the pan and let it melt.

6. Place the pancake back into the pan with the uncooked side down and cook until golden.

7. Using a spoon or spatula, break the pancake into pieces inside the pan. Continue cooking briefly until the pieces are slightly crispy.

EASTER IN AUSTRIA

Austrians celebrate Easter by dyeing eggs and going to Easter markets. The Easter bunny brings candy to children. People eat lamb-shaped cakes called *Osterlamms.*

The midnight tolling of the bells at St. Stephen's Cathedral in Vienna is one way that Austrians celebrate New Year's Eve. Families light fireworks, too. January 6 is Three Kings' Day. Children dress as the three kings, sing carols, and collect money for charity.

October 26 is National Day. All federal museums admit visitors for free. From November until the year's end, people visit Christmas markets. They shop and enjoy seasonal treats. People exchange gifts and often go to church on Christmas Eve. Austrians celebrate their **culture** and traditions throughout the year!

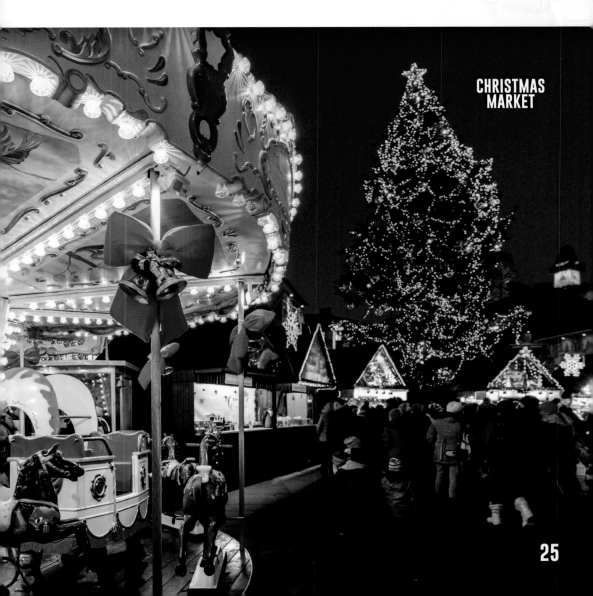

CHRISTMAS MARKET

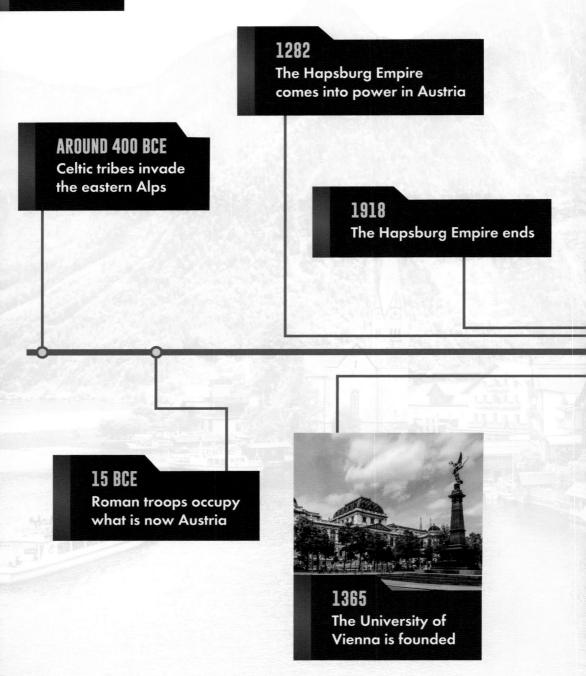

1282
The Hapsburg Empire comes into power in Austria

AROUND 400 BCE
Celtic tribes invade the eastern Alps

1918
The Hapsburg Empire ends

15 BCE
Roman troops occupy what is now Austria

1365
The University of Vienna is founded

1995
Austria joins the European Union

2021
Austria teams up with Denmark and Israel to work on COVID-19 vaccine research and development

1955
Austria becomes an independent country

1938
Germany declares Austria to be part of a union with it, called Anschluss

2019
Brigitte Bierlein becomes Austria's first woman chancellor

Official Name: Republic of Austria

Flag of Austria: The flag of Austria has three equal-sized, horizontal stripes. The top and bottom stripes are red. The middle stripe is white. According to tradition, the design is connected to a battle that happened in 1191. Flags flown by the government also have a black eagle in the middle.

Area: 32,383 square miles (83,871 square kilometers)

Capital City: Vienna

Important Cities: Graz, Linz, Salzburg, Innsbruck

Population: 8,884,864 (July 2021)

WHERE PEOPLE LIVE

COUNTRYSIDE 41%

CITY 59%

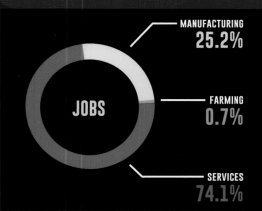

MANUFACTURING
25.2%

JOBS

FARMING
0.7%

SERVICES
74.1%

Main Exports:

cars

vaccines

medical
supplies

flavored
water

vehicle
parts

National Holiday:
  National Day (October 26)

Main Languages:
  German (official nationwide),
  Croatian (official in Burgenland),
  Hungarian (official in Burgenland),
  Slovene (official in southern Carinthia)

Form of Government:
  federal parliamentary republic

Title for Country Leaders:
  chancellor (head of government), president (chief of state)

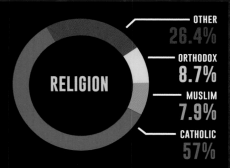

RELIGION

OTHER
26.4%

ORTHODOX
8.7%

MUSLIM
7.9%

CATHOLIC
57%

Unit of Money:
euro

GLOSSARY

apprenticeships—training positions during which a person learns a job or art from very skilled workers

continental—related to a relatively dry climate with very cold winters and very hot summers

culture—the beliefs, arts, and ways of life in a place or society

ethnic—related to a group of people who share customs and an identity

glacier—a massive sheet of ice that covers a large area of land

landlocked—enclosed by land and without access to the ocean or a sea

row houses—rows of homes which are connected by shared sidewalls

rural—related to the countryside

service jobs—jobs that perform tasks for people or businesses

streetcar—a trolley; a streetcar is a passenger vehicle powered by electricity that comes from an overhead cable.

tourism—the business of people traveling to visit other places

traditions—customs, ideas, or beliefs handed down from one generation to the next

urban—related to cities and city life

veal—the meat of young cattle

TO LEARN MORE

AT THE LIBRARY

Klepeis, Alicia Z. *The Czech Republic*. Minneapolis, Minn.: Bellwether Media, 2021.

Perritano, John. *Austria*. New York, N.Y.: AV2 by Weigl, 2020.

Rechner, Amy. *Germany*. Minneapolis, Minn.: Bellwether Media, 2018.

ON THE WEB

FACTSURFER

Factsurfer.com gives you a safe, fun way to find more information.

1. Go to www.factsurfer.com.

2. Enter "Austria" into the search box and click $\mathcal{Q}$.

3. Select your book cover to see a list of related content.

INDEX

The images in this book are reproduced through the courtesy of: Marco Wong, front cover; Mistervlad, pp. 4-5; canadastock, pp. 5 (Hallstatt, Hohe Tauern National Park), 9 (bottom); Leysanl, p. 5 (Hohensalzburg Fortress), saiko3p, p. 5 (Melk Abbey); oldnobody, p. 8; Nok Lek, p. 9 (top); iliuta gowan, p. 10 (golen eagle); Greens and Blues, p. 10 (ibex); Kletr, p. 10 (northern pike); Volodymyr Buridak, p. 10 (great bustard); Peter Fodor, p. 10 (alpine marmot); Piotr Krzeslak, p. 11; Koba Samurkasov, p. 12; Featureflash Photo Agency, p. 13 (top); Sun_Shine, p. 13 (bottom); 4kclips, p. 14; Diachuk Vasyl, p. 15; dpa picture alliance/ Alamy Stock Photo, p. 16; mauritius images GmbH/ Alamy Stock Photo, p. 17; imageBROKER/ Alamy Stock Photo, p. 18 (top), 21 (top); REUTERS/ Alamy Stock Photo, p. 19 (top); blickwinkel/ Alamy Stock Photo, p. 19 (bottom); Eva Bocek, p. 20 (top); MaciejGillert, p. 20 (bottom); givaga, p. 21 (bottom); Altrendo Images, p. 22; hlphoto, p. 23 (wiener schnitzel); JG Fotografia, p. 23 (sachertorte); AnaWein, p. 23 (kaiserschmarrn); Bestravelvideo, p. 24; Calin Stan, p. 25; trabantos, p. 26; rustamank, p. 27 (top); VfGH/Achim Bieniek/ Wikipedia, p. 27 (bottom); Lars Poyansky, p. 29 (banknote); spinetta, p. 29 (coin).